trees:
Earth's Lungs

Barbara L. Webb

ROURKE PUBLISHING
www.rourkepublishing.com

www.rourkepublishing.com

PHOTO CREDITS: Cover: © JY Lee; Title Page: © james steidl; Page 5: © Ron Chapple Studios; Page 6, 18, 19; © Iakov Kalinin; Page 7: © Irina Igumnova; Page 8, 9: © Pavel Losevsky; Page 11: © Jan Rihak, © Photohound-Wikipedia; Page 12: © Peter Wollinga; Page 13, 15: © malerapaso; Page 14: © John Wollwerth; Page 17: © Melinda Nagy; Page 20: © Alija; Page 21: © Maica

Edited by Kelli Hicks

Cover and Interior design by Tara Raymo

Library of Congress Cataloging-in-Publication Data

Webb, Barbara L.
 Trees : earth's lungs / Barbara L. Webb.
   p. cm. -- (Green earth science)
 Includes bibliographical references and index.
 ISBN 978-1-61590-304-7 (Hard Cover) (alk. paper)
 ISBN 978-1-61590-543-0 (Soft Cover)
 1. Trees--Juvenile literature. 2. Trees--Environmental aspects--Juvenile literature. I. Title.
 QK475.8.W43 2010
 582.16--dc22
                                    2010009885

Rourke Publishing
Printed in the United States of America, North Mankato, Minnesota
033010
033010LP

www.rourkepublishing.com - rourke@rourkepublishing.com
Post Office Box 643328 Vero Beach, Florida 32964

Table of Contents

Living Things Need Oxygen

Take a breath. Your **lungs** pull **oxygen** in. Your lungs push **carbon dioxide** out. Every second of the day, you need to breathe.

Did you know that trees breathe, too? Trees are the lungs of our world.

Trees breathe in the carbon dioxide we do not need.

Trees breathe out and fill the air with the oxygen people and animals need.

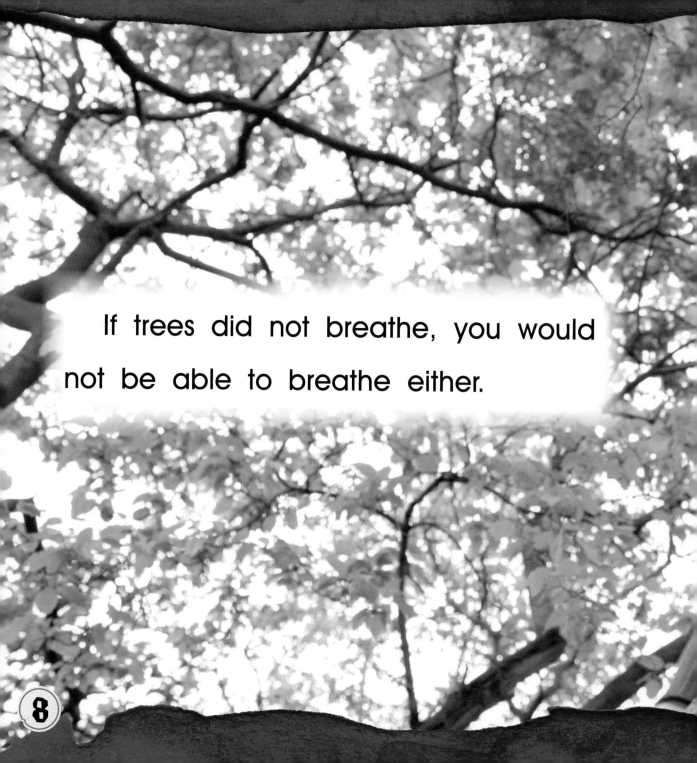

If trees did not breathe, you would not be able to breathe either.

How Trees Breathe

How does this work? Trees' leaves have tiny holes underneath called **stomata**. Stomata open during the day and breathe in carbon dioxide.

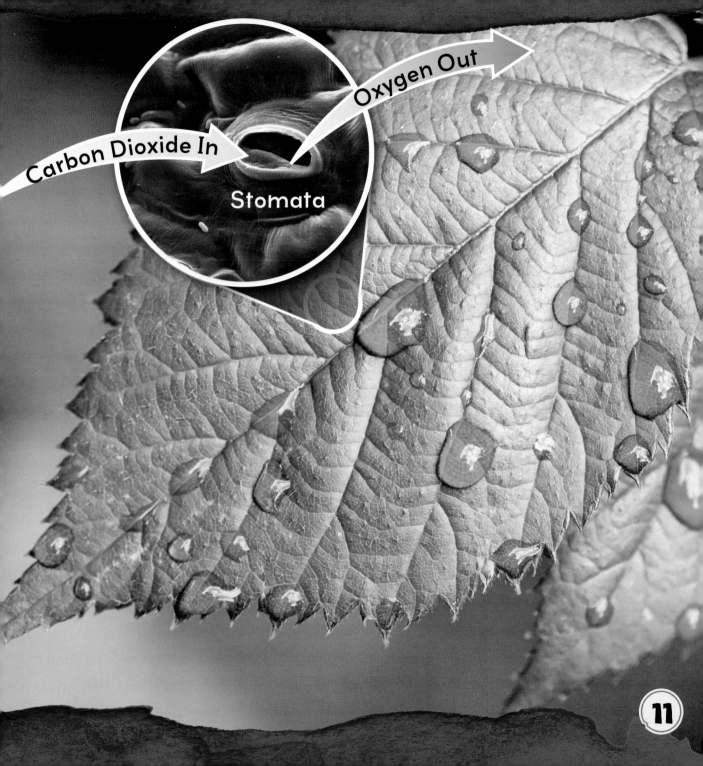

Carbon Dioxide In

Oxygen Out

Stomata

11

The tree makes food from this carbon dioxide, water, and sunlight.

Inside the tree, the Sun energy breaks apart the water and carbon dioxide. The tree turns these smaller pieces into the sugar it needs for food.

Trees in jungles are very good breathers. They get more water and sunlight than other trees so they make more oxygen.

Sun's Energy

Carbon Dioxide In

Sugar for food

Water In

The tree also has some extra oxygen it does not need. The stomata open and the extra oxygen leaves the tree. Now we have oxygen to breathe!

Fun Fact:

One fully-grown tree makes enough oxygen to keep two people alive!

Sun's Energy

Oxygen Out

Carbon Dioxide In

Sugar for food

Water In

Breathing Trees Cool our Earth

Cars and factories make too much carbon dioxide by burning gas and **coal**.

Air with a lot of carbon dioxide traps heat from the Sun. It acts like a blanket that keeps our Earth too warm.

When trees breathe in carbon dioxide, they keep our Earth cool.

We Need Trees

We need trees everywhere to keep our air cool and full of oxygen.

Planting trees is a good idea. Where could you plant a tree?

Try this:

Ask a grownup to help you with this project.

1. Place a piece of a water plant (pondweed) from a pet store in a deep bowl of water.

2. Put another jar or glass on its side in the bowl and let it fill up with water.

3. Turn the jar upside down to cover the plant. Do not let any air in.

4. Leave the plant in a sunny place.

5. In a day or two, watch oxygen bubbles rise to the top of your upside-down jar. The plant is breathing!

Glossary

carbon dioxide (KAR-buhn dy-OX-side): an invisible gas that is part of Earth's air that plants breathe in and people and animals breathe out

coal (kohl): a black mineral found underground that people mine and burn for energy

lungs (luhngs): the part of the human body used for breathing

oxygen (OX-suh-juhn): an invisible gas that is part of Earth's air

stomata (stoh-MAH-tuh): tiny holes on the bottom of plant leaves that let carbon dioxide, oxygen, and water in and out of the plant

Index

Websites

www.treetures.com/

sites.ext.vt.edu/virtualforest/

www.inhs.illinois.edu/resources/tree_kit/student/index.html

www.arborday.org/kids/carly/

About the Author

Barbara Webb lives in Chicago, Illinois with 3,585,000 trees. She grows two of them on the roof-deck of her apartment on the eighth floor. She loves writing books about interesting things kids want to know about, like presidents, recycling, and trees!